the
marriage
preparation
course

> Guest Manual

This manual is designed to be used on The Marriage Preparation Course with the DVDs or live talks. See page 48 for more information on how to join or run a course.

Published in North America by Alpha North America, 2275 Half Day Road, Suite 185, Deerfield, IL 60015

© 2009 Alpha International, Holy Trinity Brompton, Brompton Road, London, SW7 1JA, UK

The Marriage Preparation Course Guest Manual

First printed by Alpha North America in 2006

This revised edition 2010

Printed in the United States of America

Illustrations by Katy Harvey

Scripture in this publication is from the Holy Bible, New International Version (NIV), Copyright 1973, 1978, 1984 International Bible Society, used by permission of Zondervan. All rights reserved.

ISBN 978-1-934564-43-1

Contents

The value of marriage preparation

Knowing how to make a marriage work

- marriage is the most exciting and the most challenging adventure we can undertake
- strong marriages don't develop automatically
- over 40% of marriages in the UK break down
- best way to insure a marriage is to invest in it

Learning the necessary skills

- how to communicate effectively
- how to resolve conflict
- how to meet each other's emotional needs
- how to build a friendship
- how to develop our sexual relationship
- how to determine roles

Becoming aware of the differences between us

- different expectations
- our upbringing
- cultural differences

Learning to communicate

Communication involves talking and listening effectively

- process of learning how to be good communicators

Our communication is affected by:

1. Our personality
- extrovert or introvert
- logical or intuitive

Exercise

How We Communicate

Tell your fiancé(e) how you think their personality impacts the way they communicate.

---

2. Our family background
- some families air differences immediately/ others delay
- some are quiet/others are much louder
- some are more volatile/others are calmer
- some take turns to talk/others frequently interrupt

3. Our circumstances
- our job
- children
- pressures from outside and within our marriage

Barriers to effective communication

1. Insufficient time
- set aside time for meaningful conversation on a regular basis
- plan this time (it doesn't just happen)
- planned time prevents a backlog of non-communication or mis-communication
- recognize when to drop everything and listen

Exercise

Family Styles of Communication

Complete the following exercise on your own and then talk about it together.
Mark with an "x" where you think your own family comes on the line between the
two extremes.

Overall the communication in my family was:

Indirect	Direct
Vague	Specific
Relaxed	Stressful
Non-confrontational	Confrontational
Closed	Open
Loud	Quiet
Humorous	Serious

How has the way your family communicated when you were growing up affected
the way you communicate now as an adult? How different is this to the way your
fiancé(e)'s family communicates?

2. Failing to talk about our feelings

- danger of communicating only about practical things or at the most superficial level
- sharing our innermost thoughts and feelings is essential for a strong marriage
- some people find talking about their feelings difficult because of inadequacy, vulnerability, or fear
- dare to trust your fiancé(e) and start disclosing your feelings to him or her
- listen to each other without judging or criticizing

Exercise

Effective Talking

Ask your fiancé(e) how difficult or easy it is for them to talk about their inner thoughts, attitudes, and emotions. Find out if they were encouraged to talk about their feelings during their upbringing.

---

3. Holding on to hurt and resentment

- tell each other when and why you are feeling resentful
- listen and try to understand
- keep apologizing and forgiving

4. Failing to listen to each other

- listening is costly
- listening demands time and patience
- recognize and overcome bad habits such as:
  - interrupting
  - going off on a tangent
  - giving advice
- effective listening is something we can all learn and practice
- put aside your own agenda and try to see the world through your fiancé(e)'s eyes
- make the effort to understand your fiancé(e) when they think or feel differently

Exercise

Effective Listening

1. Ask your fiancé(e) to tell you about something that is worrying them. Listen carefully.
2. Reflect back what they have said, particularly about their feelings, to show that you have understood. If you did not understand, your fiancé(e) should tell you again.
3. Then ask, "What's concerning you most about what you've told me?"
4. Again reflect back what they say.
5. Then ask, "Is there anything you could do (or, if appropriate, you'd like me or us to do) about what you've just said?"
6. Again reflect back what they say.
7. Finally ask, "Is there anything else you would like to say?"

Then swap roles.

Write down your answers to the following questions and then discuss them with your fiancé(e).

1. Are you a good listener?
   On a rating of 1 to 10 score your ability as a listener:

   1 ☐ 2 ☐ 3 ☐ 4 ☐ 5 ☐ 6 ☐ 7 ☐ 8 ☐ 9 ☐ 10 ☐

2. How would you rate your fiancé(e)?

   1 ☐ 2 ☐ 3 ☐ 4 ☐ 5 ☐ 6 ☐ 7 ☐ 8 ☐ 9 ☐ 10 ☐

3. When have you had the best conversations about your deepest thoughts and emotions? Which times and places are most conducive to good communication?

   _____

   _____

4. What have been the worst times and places for communicating effectively? Can you work out why?

   _____

   _____

5. Complete the following: I find it easier to be open and vulnerable with you when you . . .

   _____

   _____

This exercise is adapted from *Looking up the Aisle?* by Dave and Joyce Ames (Mission to Marriage, 1994)

Why marriage?

- trends in our culture causing marriage breakdown:
  - consumerism
  - "throw-away" mentality
- current research shows benefits of stable marriages to individuals and society
- the biblical view:
  "For this reason a man will leave his father and mother and be united to his wife and the two will become one flesh" (Genesis 2:24)
- marriage—a vital part of God's design for human society

> Alvin Toffler, sociologist and best-selling author, wrote that people today have a "throw-away" mentality. They not only have throw-away products but they make throw-away friends and it is this mentality which produces throw-away marriages.

Two purposes of marriage:

1. Friendship

- *"It is not good for the man to be alone"* (Genesis 2:18)
- marriage isn't the only way to counter aloneness but is the closest human relationship
- marriage meets our longing for intimacy

2. Family life

- ideal is for children to grow up seeing an intimate, committed, long term relationship between their parents
- breakdown of marriage has effect on next generation
- a strong marriage can break the cycle of failed relationships

---

Exercise

The Benefits of Marriage

Discuss between the two of you: What, in your view, is the role of marriage in society? Why are you choosing marriage rather than cohabitation?

The marriage covenant

- infatuation versus lasting love
- difference between a contract and a covenant
- commitment is protective casing around our relationship
- intimacy requires vulnerability
- vulnerability requires trust
- trust requires commitment
- your wedding vows express commitment to each other

"Love and faithfulness meet together."

Psalm 85:10

Exercise

The Marriage Vows

Read through the Marriage Service vows together and decide which is the most important phrase for each of you. Explain your choice to your fiancé(e) (see Appendix 3).

Spending time together

- make it happen—through planning
- organize change of routine and do something special
- creates opportunities for effective communication
- keeps romance, love, and fun alive

Suggested ways to make time together:

1. Daily basis

- connect with each other every day
- choose best time of day
- create habits

2. Weekly basis

- "date night" or "marriage time" once a week
- plan marriage time (write it in your day planners)
- make marriage time a priority over other demands
- protect marriage time from interruptions (friends/family/telephone)

3. Annual basis

- mini-honeymoon each year
- plan vacations
- these help revitalize your relationship and rekindle romance

Exercise

Planning Time Together

Discuss when you will spend time together investing in your marriage on a daily/weekly/annual basis.

Write down your plans:

- _____

- _____

- _____

- _____

- _____

The change of loyalties

1. Leaving

- the new center of gravity—physical, psychological, and emotional leaving
- church wedding service may include symbolic leaving
- new decision-making structure
- marriage relationship takes priority
- make your own decisions and support each other

2. Respecting our parents

- showing gratitude
- staying in touch
- taking the initiative
- deciding together on level of contact
- planning for major festivals

3. Arranging the wedding

- hard work!
- an emotional process
- be prepared to compromise

"When a husband and wife have an agreed policy and stand firmly together putting it into effect, attempts at exploitation and manipulation invariably fail. But any weakness, any crack in the unity of husband and wife enables the in-laws to drive a wedge in between."

David Mace

Exercise

Parents and In-laws

Discuss as a couple:

From the following list, what possible areas of tension can you foresee with your parents/parents-in-law?

1. Vacations
2. Christmas/holidays
3. Finances
4. Interference

5. Frequency of visits
6. Length of telephone calls
7. Changed loyalty
8. Other . . .

How could they be resolved?

_____

_____

Allowing time apart

Two dangers:

1. Too much time apart
   - not enough shared interests

2. No space to pursue separate interests
   - some time apart is healthy for a marriage
   - requires mutual agreement and consent
   - brings fresh interests and stories into a marriage
   - renews our desire to be back together
   - need to find balance between time together and time apart

Exercise

Time Apart

Each write down any individual interests you expect to pursue without your fiancé(e):

1. _____

2. _____

3. _____

How frequently and how much time would these take?

1. _____

2. _____

3. _____

Write down any individual interests you expect your fiancé(e) to pursue without you:

1. _____

2. _____

3. _____

Please turn over ⇨

Exercise (continued)

How frequently and how much time might these take?

1. _____

2. _____

3. _____

Now compare and discuss your answers.

Expecting conflict

- we're different
- we're all naturally selfish
- we've moved from independence to interdependence

Handling anger

- anger is not wrong in itself
- two ways we can use anger inappropriately
  - rhinos: explode
  - hedgehogs: bury anger
- both are damaging and ineffective ways of resolving conflict

---

Exercise

Rhinos and Hedgehogs

Ask yourself if you have rhino or hedgehog tendencies when you are angry. If you are not sure, check with your fiancé(e) who may have a better idea!

Exercise

Look at Your Differences

1. Mark against each issue, where on the line your fiancé(e)'s and your own preferences lie, *e.g., N = Nicky; S = Sila*

   Do it separately and then exchange manuals.

2. Discuss how your differences can be complementary in your relationship.

For example:

Money Spend _____ S _____ N _____ Save

Vacations Adventure _____ S _____ N _____ Rest

Issue:

Money Spend _____ Save

Vacations Adventure _____ Rest

People Spend time with others _____ Spend time alone

Sleeping Go to bed late _____ Get up early

Tidiness Keep everything tidy _____ Be relaxed and
and under control   live in a mess

Disagreements Thrash it out _____ Keep the peace

TV Keep it on _____ Throw it out

Relaxation Go out _____ Be at home

Exercise (continued)

Issue:

Punctuality	Have time in hand _____	Cut it fine
Planning	Make plans and _____ stick to them	Be flexible and change plans
Organization	Organized _____	Disorganized
Decisions	Spontaneous _____	Cautious
Family	See often _____	See rarely
Friends	Long list _____	A few close ones
Music	Like it on constantly _____	Only at certain times
Talking	Talkative _____	Quiet
Change	Enjoy change _____	Resist change
Initiative	Like to initiate _____	Prefer to respond to others' ideas

Accepting our differences

- recognize and accept your differences
- differences can be complementary
- one attitude is not better or worse— just different
- can't expect to change each other
- appreciate each other's strengths
- support each other's weaknesses

Looking for solutions

Look for a solution together rather than attack, surrender, or bargain.

Six steps for resolving conflict effectively

1. Hit the "pause" button

- is this a good time? (the "ten o'clock rule")
- is this a good place?

2. Identify the issue

- take the issue that is causing conflict from between you
- put it out in front of you
- move towards each other to work on it together

3. Discuss the issue rather than attack each other

- learn to control temper
- avoid labeling, *e.g., "you always . . ." / "you never . . ."*
- use "I" statements, *e.g., "I feel hurt when . . ."*

4. Listen to each other

- try to understand each other's perspective
- take turns to talk

5. Work out possible solutions

- talk about different possibilities
- may help to write a list

6. Choose the best solution for your relationship and see if it works

- if it doesn't, try another solution
- if you can't find a solution together, ask for help

Using the Six Steps

1. What patterns of resolving (or failing to resolve) conflict did you observe in your parents' marriage?

2. What are the trigger points for conflict in your relationship?

3. What causes conflict to escalate and what helps each of you to hit the "pause" button?

4. Which is the most important of the "Six steps for resolving conflict" for each of you?

Dealing with finances

- marriage involves sharing everything
- set aside time to discuss finances
- different attitudes to finances can cause tension
- decide who will manage the finances
- recognize your different attitudes to money (are you more of a "saver" or a "spender"?)
- discover your true financial position
- calculate your joint income
- calculate/forecast your expenses
- do a budget (discuss the balance of spending/ saving/giving away)
- guard against over-spending (watch the credit card)
- discuss the repayment of any debts you have
- talk openly about your feelings
- developing a dynamic partnership requires:
  – honesty about the present
  – forgiveness for the past
  – agreement about the future

[See also: The Marriage Book, Appendix 3 "Working out a budget"]

Exercise

Discussing Your Finances

Each of you fill in your answers to the following questions and then discuss what you have put.

1. Describe your attitude to shopping (check appropriate boxes):

☐ source of pleasure ☐ enjoy window shopping

☐ like buying presents ☐ occasionally use it as escapism

☐ impulsive and sometimes wasteful ☐ only buy essentials

☐ depends on what I am buying, where and when ☐ avoid whenever possible

2. Do you worry about running out of money? yes ☐ no ☐

3. Will you have a joint bank account? yes ☐ no ☐

4. Will you keep separate accounts? yes ☐ no ☐

5. How will you balance spending, saving, and giving away?

_____

6. Will you work out a budget? yes ☐ no ☐

7. Can you keep control with a credit card? yes ☐ no ☐

8. Are you in debt? yes ☐ no ☐

If so, by how much? _____

Discuss your plans for repayment.

9. How much could each of you spend without consulting the other? _____

10. Who will manage your finances? jointly ☐ husband ☐ wife ☐

Forgiving each other

Hurt is inevitable. There is a simple but powerful process for healing:

1. Identifying the hurt

- tell your husband or wife when they have upset you

2. Learning to say sorry

- pride can make it hard to say sorry
- opens way for discussion and change

3. Forgiveness

- forgiveness is one of the greatest forces for healing in a marriage

- **forgiveness IS NOT:**
    - forgetting the hurt happened
    - pretending it doesn't matter
    - failing to confront our husband or wife's wrong and hurtful behavior

- **forgiveness IS:**
    - facing the wrong done to us
    - recognizing the emotions inside
    - choosing not to hold the offense against our husband or wife
    - giving up our self-pity

- **forgiveness is first and foremost a choice, not a feeling**
    - new feelings follow forgiveness
    - forgiveness deals with anger and resentment— although we might still feel hurt until healing is complete
    - forgiveness is a process—we often need to keep forgiving (sometimes on a daily basis)
    - we are to forgive out of gratitude for the forgiveness we have received

"Love keeps no record of wrongs."

1 Corinthians 13:5

"The word resentment expresses what happens if the cycle of blame goes uninterrupted. It means literally, 'to feel again.' resentment clings to the past, relives it over and over, picks each fresh scab so that the wound never heals."

Philip Yancey, *What's So Amazing About Grace?*

"Bear with each other and forgive whatever grievances you may have against one another. Forgive as the Lord forgave you."

Colossians 3:13

Exercise

Agree on a suitable time and place to discuss one important issue that is causing disagreement between you.

1. Identify the issue

_____

_____

2. How have each of you responded to this issue in the past?

Me _____

You _____

3. Both write down what you consider the main concern you each have regarding the issue.

Mine _____

Yours _____

Discuss what you have each written down. Take turns to talk and be sure to listen to each other's point of view without blaming or criticizing.

Please see next page

Exercise (continued)

4. Brainstorm possible solutions—do not rule out any at this stage.

i. _____

ii. _____

iii. _____

iv. _____

5. Discuss the solutions to see which one would work best.

6. Try that solution. If it doesn't seem to work, go back to your list and try another one.

Developing our friendship

1. Friends confide in each other
- no secrets

2. Friends talk to each other
- importance of meal times

3. Friends have fun together
- shared experiences lead to shared memories and stimulate conversation

---

Exercise

Building Friendship

Write out a list of the activities you enjoy doing together now. How could you make sure you are still doing these things together five/ten/fifteen years into your marriage?

- _____

- _____

- _____

- _____

- _____

- _____

Discovering each other's needs

- learn to recognize how each of you feels loved
- five ways through which we can show and be shown love:

  1. loving words
  2. quality time
  3. thoughtful presents
  4. physical affection
  5. kind actions

(Taken from Gary Chapman's excellent book, *The Five Love Languages*)

- like different languages to communicate love
- one will communicate love to us more effectively than the others
- often different for our fiancé(e)
- common to try to communicate love in the way we understand it and want to receive it
- need to learn our fiancé(e)'s love language(s)
- takes effort, discipline, and practice

Exercise

Discover Your "Love Languages"

Write down six specific occasions on which you have particularly known your fiancé(e)'s love for you.

I have known your love for me when:

1. _____

2. _____

3. _____

4. _____

5. _____

6. _____

Taking into consideration the six examples above, try to put the five ways of showing love in order of importance for you. Then consider which order you would put them in for your fiancé(e). When you have both finished, show each other what you have put.

For you Number 1–5 (1 = most important)	Love expressed through:	For your fiancé(e) Number 1–5 (1 = most important)
☐	**Words**	☐
☐	**Time**	☐
☐	**Presents**	☐
☐	**Touch**	☐
☐	**Actions**	☐

Building our sexual relationship

Sex

- communication at the deepest levels of our personality
- a vital and integral part of marriage
- given for our enjoyment not just procreation
- good sex is other-focused
- destructive outside a committed relationship
- an expression of love within the commitment of marriage
- involves the giving of ourselves to each other

"Do not awaken love until it so desires."

Song of Songs 2:7; 3:5; 8:4

"Trust is one of the prime requirements for a good sex life. When a couple trusts one another they can enjoy giving and receiving, but when one person might use the other, there is a tension."

Alan Storkey, *Marriage and its Modern Crisis*

Exercise

Sex and Commitment

Discuss and agree on your own boundaries prior to marriage.

How to build your sexual relationship

Six secrets for keeping sex alive:

1. See it as a journey

- a discovery over a lifetime
- importance of laughter
- growing in understanding of each other
- talk about expectations and any fears
- plan a relaxing honeymoon
- don't compartmentalize sex
- sexual intimacy affects every other part of our marriage
- sex is not just the icing on the cake—it's a vital ingredient of the cake itself

2. Be ready to talk

- differences between male and female sexuality
- sexual responses likely to be different
- can be difficult to talk because deeply private and requires vulnerability
- tell each other what turns you on and what turns you off
- don't leave to guess work

3. Be prepared to tackle problems

- most couples experience problems in their sexual relationship at some time
- problems resulting from abuse or other sexual trauma from the past may require professional help (ask your course leader for advice)
- other problems can usually be worked through together such as:
  - low self-esteem and poor body image
  - tiredness
  - different levels of desire
- most problems couples experience are common
  - don't bury the problem

- talk together
- read a book on sex together to help you talk
- problems do not equal failure
- seek help if necessary

4. Deal with past sexual relationships

- past relationships can cause jealousy and mistrust
- recognize if this is an issue for either of you
- be honest with each other
- resolved through talking/forgiveness/prayer
- bring closure to past relationships
- may need to destroy letters/diaries/photos

5. Discuss family planning and having children

- discuss both before you get married
- come to a joint decision
- children change the shape of a marriage relationship
- read a book about family planning (see Appendix 5)

6. Don't believe everything you hear

- avoid comparisons
- every marriage is unique
- physical relationship will change over the course of the marriage

---

Exercise

Talking About Sex

Talk together about whatever you think is important for you from this session to build a good sexual relationship.

Exercise

Making Decisions

This exercise will help you to prepare for Session 5.

In the left-hand column, write down who decided what in your parents' (or step-parents') marriage as a percentage of their influence (*e.g., 50:50 or 70:30 or 90:10*). Then in the right-hand column put your expectations for your own marriage.

Discuss what you have each put. If you grew up with one parent, only fill in the right hand column.

My parents		Decisions	Our marriage	
Father : **Mother**			**Fiancé** : **Fiancée**	
_____ : _____		Choice of new car	_____ : _____	
_____ : _____		Choice of where to live	_____ : _____	
_____ : _____		Choice of furniture	_____ : _____	
_____ : _____		Choice of crockery	_____ : _____	
_____ : _____		Choice of own clothes	_____ : _____	
_____ : _____		Choice of vacation	_____ : _____	

Please see next page ⇨

Exercise (continued)

My parents		Decisions	Our marriage	
Father :	**Mother**		**Fiancé** :	**Fiancée**
_____ :	_____	Choice of decoration of home	_____ :	_____
_____ :	_____	Choice of pictures	_____ :	_____
_____ :	_____	Choice of how to bring up children	_____ :	_____
_____ :	_____	Choice of TV programmes	_____ :	_____
_____ :	_____	Choice of food	_____ :	_____
_____ :	_____	Choice of number of children	_____ :	_____
_____ :	_____	Choice of husband's job	_____ :	_____
_____ :	_____	Choice of wife's job	_____ :	_____
_____ :	_____	Determining how money is spent	_____ :	_____

Matching our strides

Marriage provides us with greatest opportunity and greatest challenge. It involves:

1. Changing our behavior

- expecting to give more than we take
- making sacrifices

2. Being healed of our past

- we may overreact as a result of our upbringing
- need to look at our reactions and ask, "Is that reasonable?"
- change is possible
  - involves talking about our own reactions
  - involves forgiving those who have hurt us or let us down in the past

3. Letting go of unrealistic expectations

- marriage cannot meet all of our needs
- unrealistic expectations lead to a downward spiral

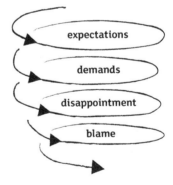

expectations

demands

disappointment

blame

4. Showing appreciation on a daily basis

- no marriage can survive lack of appreciation
- expressing appreciation of each other even when we don't feel like it

---

Exercise

Expressing Appreciation

Write a list of your fiancé(e)'s strengths and the qualities you most admire in him or her:

1. _____

2. _____

3. _____

4. _____

5. _____

6. _____

7. _____

8. _____

Then take turns reading to your fiancé(e) what you have each written.

Working out our values

- our values determine our decisions and choices
- may have different personalities but same core values
- talking about our dreams, aspirations, hopes, and longings
- putting our priorities in order

Consider the value you will put on:

1. Friendships

- enrich our lives and marriage
- all our relationships need to be redefined

2. Children

- can draw a couple closer together or push them apart
- need to keep planning time together as a couple

3. Jobs

- not competing with each other
- encouraging each other
- talking about what happens if and when we have children
- good to talk about what we hope to achieve together—to develop a vision for our marriage

Exercise

Living Out Your Values

Each of you choose your five top values and put them in order.

Then put against each one how you hope to live out that value in the future. Use the list of examples below to help you but do not be limited by it. When you have finished, compare and discuss what you have each written.

Examples of values: *health, creativity, marriage relationship, sport, vocation/ job, good stewardship of money and possessions, local community involvement, adventure, having fun, hospitality, friendships, care of environment, nurturing children, ongoing education, spirituality/relationship with God, wider family, generosity, church activities.*

Examples of how you might plan to live out a value:

• *Relationship with God: seek to pray together for each other each day*
• *Our marriage relationship: set aside time each week to have fun together*

Values:

1. _____ : _____

2. _____ : _____

3. _____ : _____

4. _____ : _____

5. _____ : _____

Creating an equal partnership

- we need to determine:
  - who does what
  - who decides what
  - who takes the lead in each area of our marriage
- assumptions from our parents' marriage
- talking about our expectations
- New Testament model
  - requires mutual giving to each other (see Appendix 2)
  - undermined male dominance
- the differences between male and female
  - which are the result of creation and which of culture?
  - male strength given to protect, not to dominate and oppress
- designed to complement each other
  - submitting to one another is key to a loving marriage

Working out roles within marriage

- who is best suited to what?
- roles will probably change over the years
- roles and responsibility

> "Submit to one another out of reverence for Christ."
>
> **Ephesians 5:21**

Exercise

Roles and Responsibilities

1. Each write down up to to six areas for which you expect to take responsibility.
   For example: housework, cleaning the bathroom, taking out rubbish, cooking, paying bills, organizing holidays, ironing, thank you letters, driving, map-reading, DIY, earning money, gardening, insurance, shopping . . .

   1. _____   4. _____

   2. _____   5. _____

   3. _____   6. _____

2. Each write down up to six areas for which you expect your fiancé(e) to take responsibility:

   1. _____   4. _____

   2. _____   5. _____

   3. _____   6. _____

3. Each write down up to six areas that you expect will be a joint responsibility:

   1. _____   4. _____

   2. _____   5. _____

   3. _____   6. _____

4. When you have finished, compare lists!

5. In which of these areas do you expect your fiancé(e) to take the lead in your marriage?

Building spiritual togetherness

As we receive from God we are able to give to each other.

"A cord of three strands is not quickly broken."

Ecclesiastes 4:12

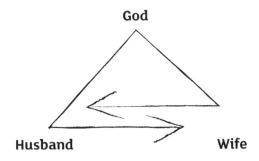

Praying together for each other can bring great intimacy.

- daily prayer—"what can I pray for you today?"
- focus on each other's needs
- accept the same requests day after day
- start with thankfulness
- praying doesn't just happen—needs to be planned

Exercise

Spiritual Togetherness

Tell each other what the diagram of the triangle above means to you, if anything, and whether you'd like to pray together regularly.

Exercise

Putting it Into Practice

Three things I especially want to remember and practice from The Marriage Preparation Course:

1. _____

2. _____

3. _____

Show your fiancé(e) what you have written.

Now ask him/her, "What three things would you especially like me to remember and practice from the course?" Write them down here:

1. _____

2. _____

3. _____

Appendix 1

Ready for marriage?

(see *The Marriage Book* – Appendix 1)

- **The sharing test**
  Do I want to share the rest of my life with my fiancé(e)?

- **The character test**
  Do I regard my fiancé(e) as being kind?

- **The strength test**
  Does our love give me energy and strength, or does it drain me?

- **The respect test**
  Do I respect my fiancé(e)?

- **The habit test**
  Do I accept my fiancé(e) as they are now (bad habits and all)?

- **The quarrel test**
  Are we able to admit our mistakes, apologize and forgive each other?

- **The interest test**
  Do we have interests in common as a foundation for friendship?

- **The time test**
  Have we weathered all the seasons and a variety of situations together?

These tests have been adapted from *I Married You* by Walter Trobisch (IVP, 1973).

If you are unable to answer yes to the questions above, we suggest you discuss your feelings with someone other than your fiancé(e).

Appendix 2

Ephesians 5:21–33

"[21]*Submit to one another out of reverence for Christ.* [22]*Wives, submit to your husbands as to the Lord.* [23]*For the husband is the head of the wife as Christ is the head of the church, his body, of which he is the Savior.* [24]*Now as the church submits to Christ, so also wives should submit to their husbands in everything.* [25]*Husbands, love your wives, just as Christ loved the church and gave himself up for her* [26]*to make her holy, cleansing her by the washing with water through the word,* [27]*and to present her to himself as a radiant church, without stain or wrinkle or any other blemish, but holy and blameless.* [28]*In this same way, husbands ought to love their wives as their own bodies. He who loves his wife loves himself.* [29]*After all no one ever hated his own body, but he feeds and cares for it, just as Christ does the church* – [30]*for we are members of his body.* [31]*"For this reason a man will leave his father and mother and be united to his wife, and the two will become one flesh."* [32]*This is a profound mystery – but I am talking about Christ and the church.* [33]*However, each one of you must love his wife as he loves himself, and the wife must respect her husband."*

1. The context of the whole passage is: "Submit to one another out of reverence for Christ" (Ephesians 5:21). (Submitting is the opposite of lording it over or seeking to control. Marriage is designed to be a relationship of mutual giving as we seek to serve each other and to put each other's needs ahead of our own.)

2. Compare the duties of husband and wife (more is written to the husband owing to the prevailing culture in which a husband had total rights over his household):
   – the husband's duty: *"Husbands, love your wives just as Christ loved the church and gave himself up for her . . . husbands ought to love their wives as their own bodies."* (Ephesians 5:25, 28).
   – the wife's duty: *"Wives, submit to your husbands as to the Lord"* (Ephesians 5:22).

3. "Head" does not necessarily mean leader. St. Paul could be emphasizing the close connection between husband and wife in marriage. They cannot act independently of each other any longer.

4. Servant-leadership means taking responsibility rather than leaving the issue to our husband or wife: we should take the initiative rather than taking control.

5. The whole passage is set in the context of seeking God's will rather than seeking to impose our own will: *"Find out what pleases the Lord . . . understand what the Lord's will is"* (Ephesians 5:10, 17).

The marriage vows

The priest/minister says to the bridegroom:
N, will you take N to be your wife? Will you love her, comfort her, honor and protect her, and, forsaking all others, be faithful to her as long as you both shall live?

He answers:
I will.

The priest/minister says to the bride:
N, will you take N to be your husband? Will you love him, comfort him, honor and protect him, and, forsaking all others, be faithful to him as long as you both shall live?

She answers:
I will.

The priest/minister may receive the bride from the hand of her father.
The bride and bridegroom face each other.

The bridegroom takes the bride's right hand in his, and says:
I, N, take you, N,
to be my wife,
to have and to hold
from this day forward,
for better, for worse,
for richer, for poorer,
in sickness and in health,
to love and to cherish,
till death us do part,
according to God's holy law,
and this is my solemn vow.

The bride takes the bridegroom's right hand in hers, and says:
I, N, take you, N,
to be my husband,
to have and to hold
from this day forward,
for better, for worse,
for richer, for poorer,
in sickness and in health,
to love and to cherish,
till death us do part,
according to God's holy law,
and this is my solemn vow.

Appendix 4

Suggested readings for your marriage service

Psalm 19, 84, 85, 91, 121, 139:1–18

Ecclesiastes 4:9–12

Song of Songs 8:6–7

Isaiah 40:25–31

John 2:1–11

John 15:1–4, 9–17

1 Corinthians 13:1–8(a)

Ephesians 3:14–21

Ephesians 5:21–33

Philippians 2:1–11

Colossians 3:12–17

1 John 4:7–16

Appendix 5

Recommended books

The Five Love Languages
by Gary Chapman (Northfield Publishing, 1995)

The Other Side of Love: Handling Anger in a Godly Way
by Gary Chapman (Moody Press, 1999)

Boundaries in Marriage
by Dr. Henry Cloud and Dr. John Townsend (Zondervan, 1999)

Look Before You Leap
by J. John (Authentic Lifestyle, 2004)

The Marriage Book
by Nicky and Sila Lee (Alpha International, 2002)

The Mystery of Marriage
by Mike Mason (Triangle, 1997)

Loving Against the Odds
by Rob Parsons (Hodder & Stoughton, 1994)

Sixty Minute Marriage
by Rob Parsons (Hodder & Stoughton, 1997)

A Celebration of Sex
by Douglas Rosenau (Thomas Nelson, 2002)

Rules of Engagement
by Katharine and Richard Hill (Lion Hudson plc, 2009)

themarriagecourseusa.org

If you are interested in finding out more about *The Marriage Preparation Course* or *The Marriage Course* (designed for married couples), where they are running or how to start up a course, please contact:

Alpha U.S.A.
2275 Half Day Road
Suite 185
Deerfield, IL 60015
Tel: 800.362.5742
Tel: + 212.406.5269
e-mail: marriagecourse@alphausa.org
www.themarriagecourseusa.org

Alpha Canada
Suite #230 – 11331 Coppersmith Way
Riverside Business Park
Richmond, BC V7A 5J9
Tel: 800.743.0899
Fax: 604.271.6124
e-mail: registrar@themarriagecourse.ca
www.themarriagecourse.ca

To purchase resources in Canada:

Alpha in the Caribbean
Holy Trinity Brompton
Brompton Road
London SW7 1JA UK
Tel: +44 (0) 845.644.7544
e-mail: americas@alpha.org
www.alpha.org

David C. Cook Distribution Canada
P.O. Box 98, 55 Woodslee Avenue
Paris, ON N3L 3E5
Tel: 800.263.2664
Fax: 800.461.8575
e-mail: custserve@davidccook.ca
www.davidccook.ca

If you are interested in finding out more about the Christian faith and would like to be put in touch with your nearest Alpha course, please contact:

Alpha U.S.A.
e-mail: info@alphausa.org
www.alphausa.org

Alpha Canada
e-mail: office@alphacanada.org
www.alphacanada.org

Alpha in the Caribbean
e-mail: americas@alpha.org
www.alpha.org

CPSIA information can be obtained at www.ICGtesting.com
Printed in the USA
BVOW08s2252240215

389176BV00002B/4/P